SAVED:

and

Surviving Single Hood

By

Kimberly Slater

Order this book online at www.trafford.com
or email orders@trafford.com

Most Trafford titles are also available at major online book retailers.

Printed in Victoria, BC, Canada.

ISBN: 978-1-4269-2548-1

*Our mission is to efficiently provide the world's finest, most comprehensive book publishing
service, enabling every author to experience success. To find out how to publish your book, your
way, and have it available worldwide, visit us online at www.trafford.com*

Trafford rev. 2/25/2010

Trafford PUBLISHING®   www.trafford.com

North America & international
toll-free: 1 888 232 4444 (USA & Canada)
phone: 250 383 6864 ♦ fax: 812 355 4082

This book is dedicated to my late great-grandmother Ida E. "Nana" Howard. Thank you for showing me strength beyond measures.

Prologue

March 22, 1996, was the happiest day of my life; no it wasn't my wedding day it was the birth of my daughter. That day changed my life; I no longer wanted to be "that girl" on the block but the best mom on the block. I married my daughter's father June 12, 1997, yeah; you guessed it, having sex before marriage. Having sex before marriage was no big deal while growing up, it was normal. Sure I had grand parents who probably would have preferred for me to wait but it wasn't enforced nor expected. I was just expected to graduate high school and be able to support myself. There was no talk about sex in my house let alone talk about waiting until you're married. My parents were married at age 17 after they had me. There it is again, sex before marriage. I guess its true cycles do repeat themselves………

The beginning

"Therefore a man shall leave his father and his mother and hold fast to his wife, and they shall become one flesh" (Genesis 2:34)

After having my daughter her father and I were married. We both were 26 years old when we got married. Yeah, of course that sounds like the perfect age for marriage and starting a family, but when you start the family before you get married there is nothing perfect about it. I left home probably 4-6 times in the first two years. We just couldn't get it together. I look back now and see just how awful that must have been for my daughter. It was obvious that we got married for all the wrong reasons. I guess it is true when the church folk say unequally yoke marriages don't last. My ex-husband and I were worldly people. I went to church and so did he on Easter and New Years Eve like most. We both had a past that neither should be proud of but our past was what we knew. He grew up in a house with both parents; I grew up in a house without parents. My mother and father were separated by the time I was 5 years old. My father dated many women and my mother hardly dated. I have to say a few of the women my father dated are still apart of my life today and I am grateful. There is a piece of each of them in me and it has molded me into the woman I am today. But, before I became this woman I was another kind of woman. Since I was a mother now and a wife, whether I could get the marriage portion correct or not I was a young adult and it was time I began to act like it. My daughter started to get older and she began to want to walk, talk and mimic me. Children are like sponges they absorb everything. They learn first from their parents every attitude or behavior we have. The thought of her doing the things that I did as a young person was horrifying. I knew that it was time to change. My ex-husband and I started to really disconnect here. He wasn't ready for change and I wanted something, I wasn't quite sure what but I knew it was something for the better.

I started to attend church with my mother. She was saved and appeared to be happy in her life and I wanted a piece of that. She spoke about Jesus Christ often and after while; I decided that I wanted to know him for myself. Now, I knew of JESUS having attended a catholic high school so I had a little religion in me I guess. There really was no reason for me not having some kind of a relationship with Jesus since my nana went to church faithfully every Sunday. My nana didn't drive she would put on her Sunday best and stand at the corner of our block and wait on the #2 bus. It didn't matter snow, rain, or shine nana was there like clock work. I don't believe she missed a Sunday until she got up in age and could not catch the bus by herself. That is one of the things I must say I regret. Now that I know JESUS for myself I wished I had known him much sooner. I remember going to church with nana maybe once or twice but no more than that. I won't ever forget the first time I walked into Deliverance Evangelistic Church on 22nd St. My mother and

I had decided that I would meet her inside where she would be waiting for me. I had never seen a church so big in my life, it was beautiful and the people were so pleasant. As I walked in looking for my mother I spotted her waiting patiently by the doors of the statuary. I remember thinking to myself, ok I think I like this. I don't know if it was the spirit of the place or the awe… feeling I got as we were walking to our seats. I felt something going on inside of me, I couldn't figure it out but it felt good. The lights were dim and there were several women kneeling at the altar, some walking and speaking in a language that I didn't understand. I was in amazement. I had never seen people praying out loud like this. I went to a catholic school and my grandmother was Lutheran while my nana was Baptist so this was different, really different. The worship team began to sing and the lights came up. The church looked even more massive than I was imagining from outside. They sang a song that is one of my favorites today. It is called "Waiting on You" by Clint Brown. Gospel singer Fred Hammond made a remake to the song today with an upbeat tempo. The worship team sang its original melody and it made my heart sink. I never forgot that song or the feeling I got that day. It felt as if the Lord was speaking directly to me. The Pastor was preaching about Godly thinking. The Pastor said in order to have godly success you must have healthy thinking. Setting our minds on heavenly things is a choice (Phil 4:8). That day I decided it was time to think of more for myself and family. My mother and I left the church at the end of service; she began to introduce me to a few of her church friends. Again, they all were very pleasant. I definitely liked the feel of this place. I decided right then and there that I would be returning next Sunday. I started on my way home and I all I could think about was how the Pastor had to be talking to me. How did he know what I was feeling? I began to think ok, what am I going to wear next week and what am I going to put on my daughter for church. This was the start of something new and it felt good just thinking about it. *"As a man thinks in his heart, so is he" (Proverbs 23:7).*

I had arrived home and began to tell my ex how I really loved the service and it felt good being there. I told him I want us to go next Sunday. Well he didn't agree right away he had some hesitation but in the end he said ok. Next Sunday couldn't come fast enough for me I just wanted to be there. I couldn't explain my sudden attraction to this church. I know now it wasn't the church it was GOD speaking to my heart. *"My sheep hear my voice, and I know them, and they follow me" (John 10:27).* Sunday morning came and we as a family went to church and it was just as good as the first time. The Pastor spoke about setting goals for ourselves. Well my mind was already wondering, like you know, girl he is right. I need to make a list of my goals. I knew the first one on the list was going back to school. I wanted to get my bachelor's degree in criminal justice. I had been thinking about it for sometime now, and it was time. I was working at the court house and just seemed to love law enforcement. I had several family members who had some type of law enforcement position. In fact my aunt and best friend had just applied to the Philadelphia Police Department to be an Officer. I thought to myself, yeah I need to go back to school. This was my first goal on the list. Today, I realize that my first goal should have been getting closer to Jesus Christ, getting Jesus to confirm if this was his plan for me. I needed to pray first! If we do anything without God we will fail. Whether in our own strength or supernatural if it is without God it will fail. *(Isaiah 41:10)* I still had so much to learn.

Service was over around 2:15-2:30 we decided to go pass his parents house so we could have dinner, which was our usual anyway. My in-laws are wonderful people. The horror stories most people speak about when it comes to their in-laws I couldn't relate, mine were really good to me. My mother-in-law is a fabulous cook and she always cooked a large meal on Sundays. If you eat her food you could forget about seconds and just move your mind right to 3rd and 4th. This isn't good for your diet but hey you only live once, right. We walked in the door and most of the family was there just sitting around relaxing. When my ex stated where we were coming from one of his cousin's cracked a joke about it. He said, "oh you went to church?" You are going to be a holy roller soon, huh! My ex has always concerned himself with what people thought of him; even today he still worries about what people think. *"If anyone is ashamed of me and my words in this adulterous and sinful generation, the Son of Man will be ashamed of him when he comes in his father's glory with the holy angels. (Mark 8:38)"* He didn't respond but the look on his face said it all. It will be hard getting him to go to church next week. Next Sunday came and I was correct my ex-husband didn't want to go. I went on to church and took my daughter with me. He tried to make me stay home with him. He started making all kinds of excuses like it's raining; she isn't going to want to sit through the service. I paid him no mind and continued to get myself and her ready for church. I was determined to go and he wasn't going to stop me. I wanted to do this and something told me I was suppose to be doing it. Service was just as good as before and my daughter fell asleep but that was ok. I just wanted her to be in the presence of the Spirit of God. We went to my in-laws after service and her father was there waiting. When I sat down next to my ex-husband he told me he would go with me next Sunday. I was rather surprised and said ok that's good. However when next Sunday came he didn't go. He began with his excuses and this time my daughter stayed home because she was a little under the weather. That was the perfect excuse for him but not for me. I was out the door and on my way to church. It became clear to him that going to church had turned into a regular thing for me on Sunday. I invited him to come on several occasions. He accepted once in a while but for the most part he didn't attend. As the months went on I began to change. I wasn't a holy roller but I was going to church, reading the bible, and praying when I had the time. Little did I know praying was to be constant not when I had time. *Ephesians 6:18 says "and pray in the spirit on all occasions with all kinds of prayers and requests. With this in mind, be alert and always keep on praying for all the saints".* Even though I was going to church I still didn't take that walk down the aisle to get saved. I am not sure what was stopping me. Probably my pride, you know looking like you got it together and having it together is totally different. If I walked down that aisle all will know that yeah I have been coming to church but I still was a sinner. I don't think I was ready for that. *"When pride comes, then comes disgrace, but with humility comes wisdom." (Proverbs 11:2)*

I woke up this morning and something about me was different. I wasn't sure what it was but something felt special. I went down into the kitchen to make breakfast and it just seemed that everything was just moving so smoothly. I knew that my ex and daughter were not going to church with me today so I didn't need to rush or get her things together. I just took my time with breakfast. I cleaned up the kitchen, took something out for dinner and proceeded upstairs and got myself together for church. I just felt so light hearted this day. I wasn't concerned about anything, everything felt RIGHT! I arrived at church at my usual time and the praise and worship felt slightly different this morning. As I looked around the church I saw the usual people in the same seats but, the room smelled different. I began to notice seats that I never noticed before. My eyes caught a glimpse of light fixtures that I couldn't remember seeing before. I sat in my usual seat closed my eyes and my hands began to sweat. I felt something coming over me. I felt as if I had no problem in the world that couldn't be fixed. All my worries or concerns were far from my mind. The Pastor for the day lesson was called "Trusting God". He preached and teached that day. He broke the bible verses down as if we were in a school classroom. Then it happened at the end of the service. He started to sing my favorite song, the song that I heard the first day I walked into this church. He sang "Waiting on You", I couldn't believe it I hadn't heard the song since the first day I stepped into the church. My heart started racing, my hands were sweating and the tears were flowing. He made the first call for those that wanted to be SAVED. I stepped out of my row and walked down the aisle. It seemed as if the walk was really long even though I wasn't that far from the altar. I was crying, sweating and shaking but my legs were still moving forward. I got to the altar and confessed my sins; and I got SAVED! *"For this my son was dead and is alive again; he was lost and is found" (Luke 15:24).*

I enrolled myself back into school and was ready for this experience. I enrolled in Community College of Philadelphia; I figured that was a good place to start. I had been out of school for 10 plus years and knew the adjustment was going to be difficult. I was only at CCP for 1 year before I started to think this isn't the place for me. I have to get out of here, I thought. The school was full of young people who really weren't ready, just playing games. I am here grown and ready, no time for games. One day I was speaking with a cousin in-law about how unsatisfied I was with CCP. She suggested trying Chestnut Hill College. She said they had an accelerated program that would be good for me. I took her advice and am very glad I did. Before the end of that month I was enrolled in the next semester at Chestnut Hill College. I didn't know at the time that this change with my educational dwelling would be so beneficial to me today. My life was rolling along so I thought. Until one day I went to church and the Pastor was preaching about being unequally yoked. My mind went straight to my ex-husband and how different are interest were becoming. He never went to church with me, he began going to dinner at his parents house without me. Now, don't get me wrong I could have gone if I wanted but we were distant with each other. We lived in the same house but it felt like we were strangers. We sat down one afternoon and attempted to have a conversation about it. We agreed that maybe we needed counseling. I was thinking you know, we may have started out wrong (fornicating) but we are married now and we need to make this work. I knew that God didn't believe in divorce so He must want this to work. My ex and I saw three different counselors in a year and half and we still couldn't get it right. I felt like he wasn't growing. He continued with worldly behaviors that I had no interest in anymore. The distance between us continued to grow and our conversation continued to lessen. Finally I told him we have to do something about this; I can't continue to live this way. We no longer lived as husband and wife, we were like roommates. I didn't have to be an expert on marriages to know that husbands and wives were not to live this way. We decided that I would move out until we could figure something out.

Divorce and single again

"To the married I give this charge (not I, but the Lord): the wife should not separate from her husband (but if she does, she should remain unmarried or else be reconciled to her husband), and the husband should not divorce his wife" (1 Corinthians 7:10).

My ex began seeing other people and I must admit it hurt at first but then I said we aren't together so why are you tripping? I then started to date as well. My ex didn't like that at all, it was ok for him but not for me. Men have another whole set of rules for themselves. I will never forget the day he came to my grandmothers where my daughter and I was staying and told me if we aren't going to be together then we should get a divorce. I told him if that is what you want then fine. I wasn't in the mood to neither fight with him nor talk about marriage. I was hurt, tired and confused about my direction at this point. I just wanted to be left alone until I could figure me out. I was continuing to attend services pay, my tithes and just live. I thought I had it all together. Little did I know the lessons that GOD was bringing forth in my life. See I didn't pray before I made the decision to leave. I never sought GOD'S approval or guidance. *Psalm 32:8 "I the Lord will instruct you and teach you in the way you should go; I will counsel you with my eye upon you"*. The divorce was a quick no-fault type of divorce. He asked for the divorce but then decided he wanted to stop it after papers were signed. I told him no you wanted this, you're getting this. Neither one of us probably really wanted a divorce but we let our pride and flesh get in the way. He had started to see other people right after we separated so I felt like we weren't married anymore anyway. Today, as I walk closer with the Lord and feast on the word of God, I know that my ex and I were still husband and wife regardless of our worldly physical circumstances. I should have been getting next to Jesus not another man. The book of Deuteronomy 8:1-6 says that the bible should be apart of our daily diet. How can we get to know GOD if we don't read about him? Just as one may study in college for midterms or finals is just how we should study GOD. When we want to interview for a job we learn all we can about the company and the position being offered. Well having a position in heaven is better than any job on earth. *Our hearts or minds are to be continuously set on these "things above" where Christ is in heaven, not on "earthly things" (Col. 3:1-4).*

Being single again had its good and bad. My ex and I arranged an every other weekend schedule for my daughter. He started out giving me money for daycare and we agreed to split everything for her until, he got a new girl friend who told him that he should give me money orders so he could keep a record. Well don't get me wrong I do understand that in some relationships this is necessary but this was once my husband and he knew what I would and would not do for our daughter. I got upset with him and told him so. How dare he let another person tell him what he needs to do when it concerns our daughter? My ex has always been the type to listen to others, almost like who ever says it first. So, in other words I shouldn't have been surprised. I began to see him in a different light that day. Then it happened, he decided it would be best if we went through the court system for a court order on support. He had spoken to one of his friends and they told him he was paying too much in support. Now, at this point he was only paying $100 dollars a week and I know I don't need to say how much daycare was weekly. Things really began to change with us when it concerned our daughter. He began to spend less and less time with her. He was now the party entrepreneur, throwing parties once a month. Complaining about splitting expenses with me because the court order said one thing and he believes that "WHAT EVER THE SUPPORT ORDER SAYS THAT IS ALL HE HAS TO DO". Anyone who has a child knows that child support goes above and beyond the court order. He took me back to court for decreases at least 5 times in one calendar year. I couldn't believe they continued to allow him to do so. He then lost another job and it was becoming ridiculous. The court said I made more than him so the numbers leveled out that way. What a system right? By the third time I decided that was it, I wasn't going to court anymore. My ex was now paying less than $60 a week. He did nothing more than Christmas and her birthday, unless his parents got involved. He was testing my patience more and more and it was wearing me down. He was telling my daughter to call his new girlfriend of 5 months, mommy. I just couldn't stand him anymore. He wasn't acting like a father or an adult. I remember thinking to myself this is why we are divorced. He is such a child. I had decided that it was me and my baby against the world. Here is yet another mistake I was making and didn't see. It wasn't me and her against the world. You can't do anything without God! I had forgotten that, I had lost my prayer life, I was losing my connection. I began to allow his ignorance to transfer over to me. I began to worry about what he was doing and not doing. I was losing ground and losing it fast. *"A fool gives full vent to his anger, but a wise man keeps himself under control"* *(Proverbs 29:11).*

At this time I got some assistance from my uncle who is a financial wiz kid. He did a budget for me without the child support added into my income. I must say it was hard to look at this budget let alone follow it, but as time went on it got easier. Actually having a budget; I was much more mindful about frivolous spending. My ex noticed that I didn't ask him for money anymore. My mind was made up whatever he did for my daughter would be extra. Later that same year I found that he had another child who was a year younger than my daughter. Now, I always thought my ex cheated on me but now I knew for sure. You know they say women are born with intuition; I must say I believe it now. I remember questioning him about infidelity and of course he denied it. But today my assumptions were proven correct. The day I found out I questioned him about it, and I am not even sure why. I guess something inside of me just wanted to know. He says she was a co-worker and he couldn't even remember the night. After he told me I wasn't even sure what I was feeling. He and I were divorced and had been for sometime so it shouldn't have mattered but for some reason, I needed to know. The little girl is 12 years old today and he continues to pay child support but he has no relationship with her. My daughter has questioned me on more than one occasion for answers but I told her she will have to ask her father. She said I did and he continues to lie to me or tell me he will get her when she turns 13. I remember one night my daughter said to me, if that was me I wouldn't want to see him after all this time and he didn't try to see me. Children are little people but they are people with feelings, issues, emotions, stress, etc. *"Train a child in the way he should go, and when he is old he will not turn from it" (Proverbs 22:6).* Speaking of my daughter, she has a love for writing poetry. I have encouraged and challenged her to write one poem a week. As I read some of her poems I see her pain in words with her relationship with her father. I only wish that one day he looks at her and really sees her before it is too late. This is the part that I didn't imagine I would have to do alone. My daughter has two biological parents but only one physical parent. It is hard being a single mother physically, emotionally and spiritually, it is challenging. You want to be strong for them in all three of these areas but if you don't have the guidance of God you will be weak. *"If the spirit of him who raised Jesus from the dead dwells in you, he who raised Christ Jesus from the dead will also give life to you mortal bodies through his spirit who dwells in you" (Romans 8:11).*

Since the divorce I managed to keep very busy. I was working, going to school and being a parent; be mindful that I said all worldly things. I was working on Sundays and left no time for God. I made sure my daughter and I had family night once a week. It normally was a night that I didn't have class or the Thursday before she went with her father. I am thankful that it is something that still goes on today. Now, it includes a few others but the tradition still lives on. We are home rather than in the street, playing board games and having theme food nights, like Mexican, soul food, Chinese or Italian. It is a wonderful time for my daughter and I to talk about what's going on with her, just simply enjoying each others company. Having a relationship with your children is very important. God is our father and He wants a relationship with us. *"For God so loved the world that he gave his only son so that anyone who believes in him should not perish" (John 3:16).* Having a relationship with Jesus is imperative if you want to have a relationship with God. This is something I know today but how many mistakes did I make in learning this lesson.

Being a single mother is hard work. Going to work everyday, having to come home and cook dinner, do homework, hers and mine. I take my hat off to women with more than one child to raise. I remember watching my nana do hair in her beauty shop in the basement of the house as a child. My nana was tuff, you hear me; I mean tuff! She was up at the crack of dawn making coffee, frying salt pork and letting customers into the basement. She gave us our bath, my aunt and I, put us in the bed and then washed her stockings out and got her dress ready for the next day. Well I found myself as a single mother doing everything systematically also. My daughter continued to grow and her needs began to increase. I was working two jobs but I felt the need for a break. I thought to myself, I can stop for about 6 months and then go back. My body needed a break; besides, I needed to get myself back to church. I had allowed my worldly obligations to take me over. I had strayed away from fellowship and it was time to get back. Besides, I missed going to church. Sure I did pray every night before I went to bed, if you call praying while lying down with a text book on my chest. I had stopped being diligent about sending my tithes and offerings into the church. I had been away from the church too long. At one time I thought maybe God was mad at me, that is why it felt like my ex was winning and I was losing. He was partying and getting his hustle on and it appeared like he was on top of the world. I was struggling to raise my daughter and he was loving life. This time I prayed about my situation and by the morning I had an answer. I realized that God was still listening to me. I still had Christ in me and I knew it, and it was time to show him. *"Who shall separate us from the love of Christ? Shall tribulation, or distress, or persecution, or famine, or nakedness, or peril, or sword" (Roman 8: 35).*

I resigned from my part time job, giving them a two week notice. The first weekend off I returned back to church. There was the Pastor sitting in the pulpit. I couldn't wait to hear the word. I realized at that moment just how much I missed it. He wasn't preaching that morning but it was ok. I was happy just being there. A few weeks went by and I was there every Sunday. My daughter was with me unless it was her father's weekend. At this time it appeared to be a lot going on in the church. I didn't want to lose the ground I found myself gaining. I couldn't explain the feelings I was having but I felt myself getting control over my life. As the weeks went on I decided that I needed a home church of my own. I had never joined this church, I was just attending. I found out later that there are many people who attend churches but never actually join. People have a hard time with commitment. There is a lack of commitment in churches and according to *John 12:18* people come to Jesus seeking curiosity or self-gratification for themselves. By the end of that month I had made a decision to follow one of the Pastors to his new church. I joined this church and it was my first time ever being a member of a church. I went to catholic high school and attended a Lutheran church on occasion but I never joined a church that I could call "my church". The church was small but the Pastor was electrifying. I was attending services every week and even went to bible study when I didn't have class. Six months went by fast and it was time to get back to having part time employment. My education was almost finished and I needed to pay for some additional classes out of pocket. My financial aid and student loans were coming to an end and adding up at the same time. I found myself another part time job in my field of study so any internship hours would qualify if needed. Before the interview I prayed about it and I asked God what should I do? I asked God for the favor of not working Sundays or be allowed to work every other Sunday. I went to the interview and I must say I felt very confident this day. I assumed in the natural realm that they would tell me no and this position was for weekends only (which would include Sunday). But, I was now thinking in the spiritual realm and I believe that God would give me favor. Well I was correct. Not only did I get the job but the position was for every other weekend and I would make the same money that I would have made working every weekend elsewhere. This allowed me to receive the extra finances I needed and also have my weekend with my daughter.

Everything seemed to be going well. Before I knew it a year had gone by and I was still feeling as if I was gaining ground. Notice that I am speaking as if this is a race. I have learned that life is just that if we allow it to be. Now, don't get me wrong, we must run from the enemy but at some point we have to stand and fight. *"Put on the whole armor of God, that you may able to stand against the wiles of the devil"* *(Ephesians 6:11).*

One foot in the church and **One** foot out!

"Examine yourselves, to see whether you are in the faith. Test yourselves. Or do you not realize this about yourselves that Jesus Christ is in you? Unless indeed you fail to meet the test!" (2 Corinthians 13:5)

It is a typical Sunday I walked into the sanctuary and the worship team was singing, the lights were dim, everything seemed normal. I began to look around at the same people I saw every week, but for some reason it was different. I noticed all the couples in the church that Sunday. Now, these are the same people who were there every week. Why didn't I notice this before? I found myself looking at their fingers to see if the wedding finger held a ring. Was I the only single person here? I am sure I wasn't but that is how I felt. All of a sudden everywhere I looked there was a couple, married or not but a couple. I began to think about my marriage failing and being alone. I never had this feeling before, why now? I began to think with could've, should've, would've syndrome. Before I knew it, I was consumed with it. I wasn't paying attention to the worship team or the presence of God. The Pastor began to preach and I didn't hear him. My body was there but my mind was some place else. I started feeling sorry for myself. I remember I started to cry and I couldn't stop. I am not sure what happened throughout the entire service but I do remember the Holy Spirit awakening me at one point so I could hear what the Pastor was saying at that very moment. The Pastor went from one side of the pulpit to the other and his physical appearance got my attention. He said "Stop looking at the picture and see the picture". *"So we fix our eyes not on what is seen but on what is unseen. For what is seen is temporary, but what is unseen is external"* (2 Corinthians 4:18). For example, if you see your bills in one hand and not enough money in your other hand, don't look *at* the bills, *see* God. He said everything that you see isn't always what it is. My spirit began to speak to me; I began to think about when my ex came to church with me. Our picture looked good but it wasn't good. Now, I am not saying that the couples there were unhappy but I can't say that they were either. My point is I needed to stop looking; it wasn't for me to see. I am grateful that the Holy Spirit didn't allow me to leave with those awful feelings. Yes I was married, yes it didn't work, but no, it doesn't make me who I am. *1 John 3:2 says "Dear friends, now we are children of God, and what we will be has not yet been made know. But we know that when it appears, we shall be like him, for we shall see him as he is".*

I left church with a different kind of feeling that day. I realized that day I was a SINGLE woman. I knew it wasn't a bad thing however; I saw me differently that day. I got home and made dinner for myself and waited for my little girl to come home. I can't lie and say I didn't think about my experience in church most of the day. My emotions went back and forth; one minute I wanted to be with someone and the next I was good by myself. My mind was starting to play tricks on me. The enemy was trying to work his mojo and it was working. My mind was playing tennis like Venus and Serena Williams for the championship. It was awful! I couldn't get a handle on them at all.

By the weekend I was making plans to go out and hit the street. At first I went to visit some old friends and you know that's how it all begins. That circle of friends you walked away from suddenly appears and the life they have seems to be better than yours. Notice, I said seems to be. After a few weeks of hanging with them we all made plans to go out for someone's birthday. Now, I have never been a bar girl anyway so I don't know what made me think that I could stomp with the big dogs as Martin would say. I was so out of place that night it wasn't even funny. I really shouldn't have been there; I had nothing in common with them anymore. These were friends I out grew and never should have looked them up again. Sure seeing them in the street in passing is one thing but thinking I would be able to hang out with them again was something totally different. I was so angry with myself that night and just as I was about to make an excuse to leave, this guy comes over and asked what I was drinking. Well, I wasn't drinking anything because I don't drink. I told him ginger ale is all. He began to joke, like you're at a bar, not a restaurant. I said yeah, I know where I am and I should be leaving. He said, oh don't leave, I was just joking. I said I wasn't, this isn't my thing at all. He said you don't drink? I said no, not really. I mean I have had a drink or two in the past but this really isn't me. He and I began to talk and the conversation was actually good. In my relationship today with the Lord I know that the enemy sends people your way that don't necessarily look like the enemy, but later you find out they were just there to get you off the track that God has for you. *"Be self-controlled and alert your enemy the devil prowls around like a roaring lion looking for someone to devour"* *(1 Peter 5:8).*

So I began dating the guy I met in bar that night. It wasn't two weeks when he began to show who he really was, a LOSER. He was a bar fly; you know the kind, a regular; where the bar maid knows what he wants to drink before he even opens his mouth. I should have noticed that the first night. I probably did but ignored it, because that is what we do. We are funny creatures. When we want something that we know isn't good for us we ignore the signs or make excuses, and when we don't want something that is good for us, we search for reasons not too. I quickly ended that friendship, but now I was feeling like I could test the waters. I was in the world of the dating scene. Again, notice what I said "in the world". I was headed for disaster and didn't even know it. Then again I knew it because I knew what God had for me. I had already had a taste of him, sure I was a babe in my spirituality but that didn't change the fact that I knew better. I knew being in the world wasn't the place to be. People who don't believe in Jesus questioned how he speaks to us. *"Behold, I stand at the door, and knock; if any man hear my voice, and open the door, I will come in to him, and will sup with him, and he with me"* *(Revelation 3:20).* I was headed down the wrong path, I felt Jesus in the bar that night. The uncomfortable feeling of being there was the Holy Spirit and that fool coming over was the enemy distracting me. I continued to attended services and pay my tithes but I felt empty. I attended family functions and went to social gatherings with unsaved people. People who did not have church on their minds, let alone Jesus. I continued to date when asked, but they never lasted more than three months. I was out in the world. It was quite amusing at first because as soon as I told the male of the month that I was celibate, they did 1 of 2 things; either they stuck around because they thought they were going to break me down or they just stepped off altogether. After the amusement I started to get angry. I couldn't believe they were acting as if sex was everything in a relationship. Then I remembered just a few years ago, so did I. It took me sometime to realize that being angry was hurting who? They didn't care that I was angry. And why was I angry? I shouldn't have expected them to feel what I felt. I shouldn't have expected them to know God. I wasn't really acting as if I knew God. Sure I had one foot in the church but the other was obviously out. It was time that I accepted that I couldn't live in both worlds.

I just wasn't growing anymore at my present church. Now at first I thought it was me, because I was still fighting the direction the Lord had for my life in some instances. I played it off a lot. I was only playing myself because God knew all the time what direction I was going. I started thinking about changing churches and then decided that leaving the church wasn't the answer. The empty feeling continued even though I was still in church. It felt as if I was at a stand still. I telephoned a dear friend of mine. I met her through her son back when he and I dated. We were in our early twenties. She and I remained friends and I could always go to her for advice if needed. She always would say she wished her son and I had made it, but that wasn't what the Lord had in mind so she would have to just love me from afar. I always thought that was special. I told her about my feelings of not growing in my present church. She explained to me that sometimes that happens. It may be time for me to move to the next level in Christ and that just isn't the place for me to do it. She also told me that I can't live in both worlds; I have to make a decision. She said I was an intelligent person and I didn't need anyone to tell me what I needed to do; I already knew what to do. *"For if we go on sinning deliberately after receiving the knowledge of the truth, there no longer remains a sacrifice for sins" (Hebrews 10:26)* She invited me to come to church one Sunday and I said sure, maybe I will start to visit some churches and see what happens. I didn't take her advice right away, I went and visited another church in south Philadelphia and thought for a moment that this is the church. It wasn't! Sure the Pastor was good but it was a Baptist church not Evangelistic and I missed that free feeling of letting God just come in and not be ashamed. *2 Timothy 3:5* says *"having the appearance of godliness, but denying its power. Avoid such people".* I didn't need to be in control or feel as if I needed to hold it together in order to be accepted. You know in some churches you have to play it cool and stay composed or you're looked at funny. I needed to be in a place where that didn't matter. Being cute, calm, cool and collected for Christ wasn't a criteria. In fact I can remember seeing people cry and get downright ugly but they let Christ in and got set free. This wasn't the place for me and I found myself once again feeling the need to find a church where God could speak to me. *"For where two or three come together in my name, there am I with them" (Matthew 18:20).* I decided that it was time to pray about this. I should have prayed about it long ago, but as usual we try to fix things without the guidance of God. I could have had my answer and direction long ago if I had taken the time to ask Jesus.

I'd telephone my dear friend again and she told me about a New Year's Eve service that they were having at her church. I will never forget that night. I took my daughter with me to the service and it was incredible. My daughter loved it and so did I. I felt something magical again. Almost like Deliverance church on 22nd St. I started thinking to myself ok this is the church but I didn't want to get too excited because I have felt that before. Even though I felt something a little different, I stopped myself and said, no just wait and see. I decided to visit the church again for their early morning service. I thought to myself, I can go to the early service and still get back home early enough to take a nap before work. The service was just as good as the first time. The Pastor didn't preach that Sunday, an Evangelist did and she brought the house down just as good. I really enjoyed the service but I especially liked the Greeters when I came into the church. They all were so warm and friendly. I started thinking to myself, if I join this church I want to be a Greeter too. Then it hit me! I have never wanted to be apart of any ministry in a church before. I wanted to belong to a church but not necessarily get involved. I thought to myself, yeah this is the place. I continued to attend this church on Sundays and I really enjoyed being there. I decided that I needed to pray first about joining. I started praying on this church everyday until I got an answer. Well, I got my answer and I joined that church and it is my church today. I have been a member now for two years. Every week since I have been there I see myself growing. I listen intensely when the Pastor is speaking. I take notes as if I am in school again. I go home and do what the Pastor would call our "homework assignment". I finally realized that, this is it. I actually see it. I see Gods love for me. I see my growth, and I like what I see. I am ready to move on to the next level in Christ. I really didn't need the world, I needed Jesus and that is all I ever needed. *"Humble yourselves, therefore, under God's mighty hand, that he may lift you up in due time. Cast all your anxiety on him because he cares for you" (1 Peter 5:6-7).*

Waiting on the Lord

"Keep yourselves in God's love as you wait for the mercy of our Lord Jesus Christ to bring you to eternal life" (Jude 1:21).

The Christmas holidays were coming and I still had shopping I needed to do for my daughter. I was working both jobs, going to school and trying to finish this semester with a good GPA before winter break. I really needed a break too. I couldn't wait to finish school I only had a few more semesters to go and I would have my Master's in Science. I should be excited but I wasn't feeling that at all. I just wanted to finish, I was tired. My graduation was set for May 2009 and it seemed so far away a few months ago but it was approaching and approaching quickly. My special project (thesis) was literally draining me. I did my thesis on "Children with HIV/AIDS". It dissected me inside and out. I had no idea how much this topic would effect me. I was running around so much I wasn't eating nor getting the proper rest. I figured I would be on vacation from school and work at the end of the month so I could catch up with my rest at that time. I also had planned to have foot surgery during my vacation. I asked myself are you sure you know what you're doing? I attended services every Sunday and that seemed to give me the strength that I needed to pull this mountain of pressure I was feeling. My Pastor was on the money every Sunday and I needed him to be. His sermons are not just preached to you but he teaches when he preaches. He breaks it down like we break down a cooking recipe. He does it step by step. *"Obey your leaders and submit to their authority. They keep watch over you as men who must give an account. Obey them so that their work will be a joy not a burden, for that would be of no advantage to you" (Hebrews 13:17).* I honestly must admit having a relationship with Jesus and knowing that he would carry me if needed, made me continue to press on.

I finished my semester and now was out for winter break. I had my foot surgery and it seemed to have been a success. I was on crutches but it was over and I had two weeks to recuperate. A close friend of mine from high school really supported me through this ordeal. It is great when you have a support system. I appreciate my mother for all that she has done for me. Her agreeing to rent from me when I decided to purchase my duplex was a huge blessing. I guess the duplex was a blessing in more ways than one. With my mother living downstairs from me it allowed my daughter to be in her own bed while I was in school. If I needed her help while recuperating she would be right there. My daughter enjoyed her Christmas presents and her smiling that morning was really all I needed. Her father telephoned and said he would be there to pick her up at two o'clock, but of course he was late as usual and he didn't get there until three-thirty. This was normal behavior for him and it wasn't worth saying anything to him about it. My daughter was upset but as mother's always do; I made an excuse for him and told her that it is the holidays and he probably had to make a few stops before coming here. She wasn't trying to hear what I was saying but she accepted it and we started to play a card game while we waited. He finally came and picked her up and now I was home alone. My mother was at work but even if she was home she would be in her place and I would be in mine. All of a sudden I started to feel bad. I was alone on Christmas day. I had been alone on Christmas before, so why was I all of a sudden feeling lonely. I got a few Christmas phone calls and watched plenty of Law & Order SVU to last me a lifetime. I took a nap and my mother came home; she woke me to let me know she would be downstairs if I needed her. I was up for the rest of the evening. I began to feel sorry for myself. I said this is ridiculous Kim you are healthy and blessed. You have some peace to yourself and you should be happy about it. I got my book bag and started working on my thesis. I said I might as well use some of this time to get some work done. I thought it would be good for me to take my mind off being by myself.

Well, school was back in session and it was one of those days. I was no longer on crutches but still wearing that horrible looking surgical shoe. When you are rushing trying to get to one place or another limping along takes you much longer. The doctor said I had at least another week before he would put me in a sneaker, so I just better make do. I decided this day that I was going to join a gym. I didn't feel as if I needed to loose weight I just enjoyed the gym when I did go in the past. I needed some place where I could physically release unwanted pressure/stresses. Now I have no idea where I was going to find the time but I said to myself what I always say to others "we make time for the things we want". I went over to Bally's gym as it was across the street from my house, can't get anymore convenient than that. I saw a commercial during the holidays for no-contract membership, so I figured that would be good because I don't want to lock into a contract. I went over and toured the gym with my surgical shoe on, imagine that. I explained that I would be able to work out in a week, of course taking it slow in the beginning. It would be good for my physical therapy also. The doctor took me out that shoe and put me in my sneaker. I started therapy and the gym at the same time. My first couple of visits to the gym was ok. You know the guys were standing around acting as if they are lifting but they are really watching the women. I didn't want to go to a co-ed gym for that reason particularly but Lucille Roberts wasn't offering no-contract membership at the time.

I'll remember this day for the rest of my life. I actually had my first break-through. Sure I had experience being in the Lord's presence a few times, but nothing would compare to this. It was one of those days. I was at work and the phone was non-stop. I was grateful that I didn't have school this night. I was exhausted from working my part time job Sunday night 3-11 and then up early at work on Monday. I needed to find the energy from somewhere because I had homework and plenty of reading that needed to get done before class the next day. I got a call from my daughter's orthodontist letting me know the cost of her braces. My insurance was only going to pay $1000.00 dollars towards them, which means the balance was on me. I really couldn't afford another bill being added to my monthly bills but, what was I going to do. The child needed braces and she is my child. I pondered the new expense and decided I was going to call her father and ask for some help. I thought he and I could split the monthly payment, which would be $75.00 dollars a piece. Well why did I do that? He told me he wasn't going to be able to do that. I said to him what are you serious? He said he already gives me support for her and he couldn't do anything more. I said you won't be paying this by yourself, I have to pay also. In fact I pay more for her than you do already. Do you know how many times I have to go into my pocket for extras for her? That little support you give helps but it doesn't put a dent in what has to be done for her. I found myself arguing with him. I was so upset and at work. I started crying and just hung up the phone. I went into the bathroom to get myself together but my day was now ruined. *"Do not to make friends with an angry man. Anger can be contagious and if we allow someone else's anger to effect us we have now swallowed poison. This can destroy the body and soul of an individual"* (Proverbs 22:24-25).

I continued with my work day but the damage was already done. I had been crying at work and my co-workers knew something was wrong. I tried to focus on my work but it was extremely difficult. I just couldn't get his voice out of my head. I couldn't understand why he wanted to mistreat my daughter. If he thinks not doing for her is hurting me, he is only kidding himself. I finally got off of work and I was glad. All I wanted to do was crawl into bed. As I walked into the house my daughter hit me with another class trip slip somewhere and the cost was $25.00. Then she said, she had another project and needed a large poster board. Before I knew I turned around and screamed at her. Telling her I didn't want to hear another word about what she needed. I asked her did she think I had a money tree outside. I went into my room and slammed the door. I hadn't even gotten out of my coat. I started walking around the room trying to take my clothes off and the tears just started rolling. I fell to the floor and just cried. I couldn't stop crying and didn't want to. I felt helpless. I asked God, why me? I am doing everything that I am supposed to do. What am I going to do now? I have enough bills on my back as it is. Every time I turn around I have to spend money for something else. Why won't he help me? Why is he doing this? Why are you not helping me? I questioned God! I just laid there crying and feeling sorry for myself. I was alone in my room but yet I felt crowded. I felt like I wasn't going to make it. My body was shaking and sweating, my neck and hands felt clammy. I screamed Jesus, I am tired! I need help I can't do this by myself anymore. When am I going to get some help too? Where are you? I need you and I need you now. That day all the emotions that I had trapped inside were coming out. I wanted to know why, why, why? I asked Jesus when is it my season. I then felt alone. I felt as if I was drowning. I stayed there on the floor for quite a while. Then all of a sudden, I remember my nana words to me when my marriage ended. She said, ok you've cried enough. Get up and move on. You have a daughter to raise. You have to survive for her and yourself. Get up from there don't cry anymore. You are not weak, you are stronger than this. It is ok to hurt. This is one of life's lessons. You will be fine, you can do this. I got up and stood in the mirror, wiped my face and walked out the room. I told my daughter to come here and sit next to me. I told her I was sorry! I explained to her that I didn't mean to yell at her and she did nothing wrong. I explained that I had a bad day but that doesn't mean I should come home and take it out on her. I assured her she could go on her trip and I would get the poster board that was needed for her project. She asked me, was I alright? I told her, I will be.

I felt better but not great. I started dinner; checked my daughters' homework, got my things ready for the next day, then got into the bed to do some reading for school. My daughter went to bed at nine o'clock, her usual time. I read a little then turned the TV off and just laid in the bed. I looked up at the ceiling and began speaking to God. I had a different tune this time. I told Jesus that I believed in him with all of my heart. I know that I was not perfect but I was striving for perfection. Lord, I am sorry I fell short today. I pray that my daughter's father one day finds himself in relationship with you. I told Jesus I want to walk the path that he has for my life and not the one that I may think I want. I thanked him for his guidance and protection thus far because my life could be different. I am blessed and I thank you. I felt myself begin to cry but the tears were different this time. They felt like sweet tears, not like the tears I had earlier. Those tears were of pain and these were of joy. I told Jesus I can do this with you, I know I can. *"I can do all things through Christ that strengthens me" (Phil 4:13).*

Patience can be blissful

"I waited patiently for the Lord; he turned to me and heard my cry" (Psalm 40:1)

I woke up the next day and felt brand new. I guess I needed that cry and conversation with Jesus. I went to work and a few co-workers asked was I alright today. I told them I will be fine. I decided I would go to the gym right after therapy this day. I had my gym bag ready to go. My work day went by quickly and smoothly. Therapy wasn't bad. My foot was getting its flexibility back which meant my walk was coming back. I tell you limping can slow you down and besides it isn't good for your posture. I walked into the gym this day and as I was walking I notice this guy watching me walk towards the ladies locker room. I thought to myself, oh he's attractive, I haven't seen him before. I went on into the locker room, changed and got myself ready for my workout. Since the locker rooms were in the back of the gym and the treadmills were in the front; I had to walk through the weight area. As I was walking, the guy was sitting there smiling at me. He said hello, I nodded my head, smiled and kept on walking. I thought to myself as I walked by oh, yeah he is cute. I got on the treadmill and had my one hour workout and was ready to go. I saw him watching me as I walked by again. I thought to myself, he probably looks at everyone that walks by.

I got home and since it was family night, we all watched a movie and ordered cheese steaks and fries. I was sitting on the sofa and for a moment I thought about the guy in the gym. I said Kim please; you don't even know this man, why are you thinking about him. I wasn't going back to the gym this week because I only went two or three times a week and today was Thursday. However, it was crazy; I felt something but didn't know what. My daughter was due to go to her father's this weekend but it didn't matter, I was scheduled to work both days as usual. It really seemed as if I didn't have a life sometimes but it was a new year and it was an exciting year ahead for me. I was going to graduate this coming May with my Master's. I actually started to get excited about it. I can't believe the year was finally here. I would be walking down that aisle in a matter of months. When I decided to get my Master's I did it for myself. Sure I went back to school initially to better myself and provide a better life for my daughter and me, but once I completed the Bachelor's I really didn't need to continue. I wanted to do this for me this time. This has been quite a journey, but a worth while one. When I think back to the beginning when I first decided to go to school to where I am now, sometimes I still can't believe it. The Lord guided me to school and with his help I persevered. *"Blessed is the man who remains steadfast under trial, for when he stood the test he will receive the crown of life, which God has promised to those who love him"* (James 1:12).

I walked into the gym and there was that guy, smiling at me. He didn't know it but I was actually looking for him.

As I was walked by him he said hello, I said hello how are you and kept it moving. I went into the locker room and thought to myself, ok you didn't come to the gym to get hooked up, besides you know these guys are here just for the hook up. I came out the locker room and walked towards the treadmills. Again, there he is looking while he is supposed to be lifting. I walked by and he smiled and so did I. I got on the treadmill and did my hour and was out. I never do more than an hour in the gym. I am not a gym junky by far. I got home and did my usual, homework mines and my daughters, dinner and then preparing for the next day. However, I found myself thinking about the guy in the gym. I said to myself, what is wrong with you girl, you don't even know this man. Why are you thinking about him so? I got into bed that night and began to think about how long I had actually been without a mate. It was quite a long time now. I haven't been in a serious relationship in two years or more. I hadn't been on a date in over a year. I probably wouldn't even know how to act. Time really flies if you aren't careful. In this case my time was flying by for the better. This time I got the opportunity to get closer to Jesus and stay focused on my daughter and my future. Relationships are work. They are almost like having another job; and I don't need another one of those. I thought to myself, well you won't be going to the gym tomorrow because you have class, so just get it together, besides he probably has a woman and will lie and say he doesn't, Men!

To my surprise, I walked into the gym this time and he wasn't there. I actually was somewhat disappointed. I thought oh well, won't see him today. I got changed into my gym clothes and started out the locker room. As I was coming out there he was sitting right in front at the first weight machine. He said hello, how are you? I said fine and yourself. He replied better now. He was smiling while saying this. I thought to myself oh boy here we go. He wants me to believe he is better now seeing me, yeah right. I got to the treadmill and said to myself, crazy, he may not be talking about you, he may be better because he finally made it to the gym. I laughed to myself. I started my workout and began to think about all that I needed to do this evening. I had a meeting at church tonight with the Greeters and Usher ministry plus it was bible study tonight. I wanted to go to bible study; I enjoyed it but I stopped for a few weeks because of my studies and school schedule, so whenever I had the time to go, I wanted to go. While I was working out completely oblivious to my surroundings, here is the guy standing next to me. He says to me, "Did you call me?" I looked at him and said, no. I thought to myself why would I call you, I don't know you. We looked at each other and started laughing. I said boy that was corny. He said I had to find a way to say something to you. Well that was the start of something wonderful. He walked along side of me the entire time while I worked out. I was thinking to myself, this guy probably tried to pick up every woman here. The conversation was ok, but I wasn't really paying attention, just listening. He then said something that got my attention. He said he always puts God first before anything else. I said, a man speaking about God being first. He had my undivided attention at that point. The conversation continued and we decided to go and have coffee at the diner at 66th and Broad. He said he didn't live far from there and I thought I would be going that way anyway to get to church. I agreed, we left the gym and went to the diner. I can remember what he ordered cheese eggs, grits, and scrapple. I ordered a BLT without the tomato actually because I don't eat tomatos. The conversation was all about Jesus and I just loved it. It was refreshing to speak with a man that wanted to speak about Christ. He told me about himself and I did the same. We exchanged numbers while eating and agreed that we both were glad he approached me, even though the line was corny. We left he went his way and I went mine. I drove down to the church thinking to myself, did that just happen, wow. I guess it did. *"Then the Lord God formed the man of the dust from the ground and breathed into his nostrils the breath of life, and the man became a living creature" (Genesis 2:7).* I went to my meeting and then bible study. The guy called me that night and we talked on the phone for two hours before hanging up. He called in the morning to give me a wake up call; I thought that was cute of him. I was driving to work thinking ok, Kim you don't know what is going on here. Don't get carried away, just go slow.

He called me everyday, sometimes two, three times a day. We started meeting at the gym during the week. He continued to walk around with me after he finished his workout and I was still doing mine. I found myself enjoying our conversations daily. He made me laugh and we spoke about Jesus Christ. We read the bible together over the phone every night for weeks. He asked me out to a movie and dinner date weeks ago but my schedule was crowded. I told him it would have to be when my daughter would be away plus I needed to see my schedule at my part time job. He was ok with that, he said whenever would be fine. Besides he gets to see me at the gym anyway so he was satisfied with that for now. We finally went on our date and we had a great time. He was such a gentleman. We started planning dates every other weekend when my daughter wasn't home.

I allowed him to come to my home and spend time with me there. This was good in the beginning but then it started to get emotionally complicated for me. I started too really like this guy and I felt he was starting to like me also. This relationship was so different than any other that I had in the past. I found myself trying to find something wrong with him. I kept saying this can't be real, he can't be like this. When is he going to show his true colors? One night I asked Jesus what was going on. I said Lord did you send this man to me. *"Your word is a lamp to my feet and a light to my path" (Psalm 119:105)*. I mean I think you did but I am not sure. I wish you could come down here and sit on the edge of my bed and just talk to me. I started to really feel this guy and I wasn't sure I wanted to. I had been in some crazy relationships in the past including my marriage. I wasn't interested in getting into yet another worthless relationship that I would want to forget about shortly after it started.

So now it had been a few months and this guy and I were still dating. It was very clear to the both of us that we were a couple at this point. He said to me one day, you know if this doesn't work out at least we found a good friend in each other in Christ. I told him no, if this doesn't work out we will not be friends. He thought I was joking because he then said it again. I stopped him and said NO; if this doesn't work out we will not be friends. We won't be anything! I have no time for games, I know what I want and don't want at this point in my life and I don't need anymore friends. He laughed at me and said ok, I understand. I laughed at myself that night when we got off the phone. I said Lord I hope that doesn't turn him off but I meant what I said Lord. He still hadn't met my daughter but he said he was ok with that. He said for me to take my time as long as I needed. We were definitely getting closer and the more time alone we spent together the more challenging it got. We both had our minds made up that sex before marriage was not an option. We both wanted to do this not just for Jesus but for ourselves. This would be the first time for both of us that we had a relationship with someone and sex was not apart of it. We tried not to discuss sex at all but the conversation arose every now and then. When they did we kept them to a minimal and prayed about it. I didn't want sex in this relationship at all. I had enough of worldly behaviors long before this guy and I wasn't going to ruin my relationship with Christ. Sure I am not perfect and I fell short plenty of times but when I said I had enough, I meant that I had enough. *"No temptation has seized you except what is common to man. And God is faithful; he will not let you be tempted beyond what you can bear. But when you are tempted, he will also provide a way out so that you can stand up under it".* *(1 Corinthians 10:13).*

The month of May was approaching and I wanted to have a graduation dinner party for myself. At first I didn't want this but my grandmother told me I should, she said I deserved it. My friend offered his house to have the party to cut back on the expense of renting a place. I thought that was very nice of him. He and I sat down and decided it would be something small but nice. We hired a caterer so it would be less of a cleanup for us even though it would be at home. The planning came together nicely; we actually realized we worked well as a team. It was time for him to meet my daughter. We were both nervous about this but it went rather well. She appeared to enjoy his company when he came over to the house. Our relationship continued to progress. He started to attend services with me weeks ago and he made comments here and there about how he felt about me but I never saw what was about to come at all. During the planning for my dinner party my nana had gone home to be with the Lord. It was a difficult time at first but this guy was right there with me. I couldn't believe it. He asked if he could go with me. What man wants to do that, I thought to myself. My nana was in a nursing home in Yeadon Pa at the time. I got a phone call from the home stating that she didn't have much time left. I left work and went to the home to see her. My nana was ready but she was fighting it. She was always a fighter. I told her that evening to go ahead and let go, that we would be alright. It was ok for her to stop fighting. I promised her I would take care of my grandmother for her and it was ok she didn't need to prove how tuff she was anymore. My friend was so caring. He held her hand and prayed over her body with me. He had never even met my nana before; this was his first and only time. About 20 minutes after leaving the home my cell phone rang and my grandmother said the home just called and said your nana has past. What did you say to her? I told my gramps what I said and she said, as usual everyone listens to Kimberly. My friend stayed with me that night. He slept in the living room and my daughter slept in the bed with me because she didn't want to be alone in her room. I said to Jesus you sent him to me, didn't you? He is the one. Thank you.

It was dinner party day. I was home getting ready with my mother. My daughter was at my friend's house with my father helping to decorate for the party. When we got there I went through the back door as I usually do. When I got upstairs I couldn't believe my eyes. The place was packed. It was beautifully decorated, the food smelled great and people were everywhere. This was supposed to be a small party but he invited people I didn't even know. I said to him, where did all these people come from? He said well I wanted to invite some people also. I said ok, with a shocked look on my face. He prayed over the food and the party got started. I walked around. He introduced me to a few of his friends. I was having a wonderful day. It was raining out but it was shining inside. My father said it was time for a toast to congratulate me. They had sparking cider and champagne glasses for everyone. I will never forget what happened next. He stood on the side of me and then dropped to his knees. My mouth just opened wide. I was shocked! He proposed to me in front of all my family and friends. I couldn't believe it. I just stood there and I didn't know what to say. I started crying in disbelief. My father said I was shaking but I don't remember that. I told everyone thank you for coming. Now I know why they really were there. I said when you are faithful, this is what happens. God is in the blessing business and will give you the desires of your heart when you give him yours. I then finally said yes. *"But if we hope for what we do not yet have, we wait for it patiently"* (Romans 8:25).

Let's Talk

As you know I couldn't possibly give you all my experiences in just a few pages but I hope you saw the picture that I tried to paint for you. I hope you saw yourself somewhere in this book or could relate to a particular situation and use the scripture to embed in yourself as I did. Living in this world can be challenging but living with Jesus is a better choice, than taking the chances to live without him. You can't do anything without Jesus Christ. Anyone who believes that they are doing this thing we call life without Jesus is only fooling themselves. I had to learn that the hard way. I had to say that is it, I had enough, enough was enough. But I am grateful because now I know Him for myself. Sure I am still young in Christ but I am aging well with Him. I say to all single mother's everywhere, give your heart and soul to Jesus. Fall in love with him as he loves you like no other. A mortal man is just that, a MAN. He will never compare to Jesus Christ. Love yourself more and know that you are worth the waiting. Don't allow your failures to determine who you are. Relationships will come and go but Jesus will always remain. The doing of this world does not have to be your doings. I thank my great grandmother and grandmother for showing me what I am really made of. Today my daughter's father contributes a little more than in previous years but that is because of the Power of GOD. I thank my family for giving me a support team while raising my daughter alone. For those single mothers who have no physical support team just "look up" God is all the support you need. *"I will lift up mine eyes unto the hills, from whence cometh my help" (Psalms 121: 1).*

Believe, have faith, and PRAY.

Love,

Your sister in Christ